Whispers of Grace

Stories • Devotions • Poems • Prayers

Volume 3

Florida Christian Writers Conference

Compiled by

Living Parables of Central Florida

Whispers of Grace

Stories • Devotions • Poems • Prayers

Volume 3

Copyright © 2020 Living Parables of Central Florida, Inc.

All rights reserved.

ISBN: 978-1-952369-21-6

Published by EA Books Publishing a division of
Living Parables of Central Florida, Inc. a 501c3
EABooksPublishing.com

Living Parables of Central Florida, Inc., of which EABooks Publishing is a division, offers publishing contests at Christian conferences to provide opportunities for unpublished authors to be discovered and earn publishing credits. We publish high quality, self-published books that bring glory and honor to God's Kingdom.

ACKNOWLEDGMENTS

We'd like to thank Eva Marie Everson and Taryn Souders of the Florida Christian Writers Conference for encouraging and equipping writers and speakers for the glory of the Kingdom of God. We wish to thank Cheri Cowell and her wonderful team at EABooks Publishing for giving us this opportunity. We thank our many friends and family for supporting us in our writing dreams. And most importantly, we want to thank our Lord and Savior Jesus Christ for His gifts—may this book bring you the honor and glory you deserve.

TABLE OF CONTENTS

Acknowledgments	iv
A Holy Heliotrope *Christy Bass Adams*	1
Did Mr. Rogers Say "Goodness"? *Sara C. Alsup*	3
MY SALT LIFE *Jackie Anders*	5
When You Think Your Kids Aren't Listening *Michael L. Anderson*	11
The Promise Keeper *Linda Ray Center*	17
He Didn't Push Her in the Well! *Carri Colvin*	21
Elijah Heard the Whisperer *Jeanie M. Connell*	25
Grace *Carolyn J. Fisher*	29
Call Answered *debi*	33
The Ellen Gift *Carol Moesta Hamilton*	35

Gifts of Grace   39
    Martha Rogers

Never Alone   41
    Sarah Schwerin

A Soft Landing   45
    Susan P. Sloan

Just Joy   47
    Irene Wintermyer

Can you hear it? Life often gets in the way of us hearing it—the roar of doubt, fear, and despair drown out the still small voice. But if we tune our ear to hear, it is there. Whispers of grace come to us when we lend our ear to the movements of God in our struggles, in our everyday lives, and in our hearts. May these stories, prayers, and poems create in you a desire to listen for the whispers of grace in your own life.

Florida Christian Writers Conference

A Holy Heliotrope

Christy Bass Adams

"Keep your eyes on Jesus, who both began and finished this race we're in. Study how he did it. Because he never lost sight of where he was headed - that exhilarating finish in and with God - he could put up with anything along the way: cross, shame, whatever. And now he's there, in the place of honor, right alongside God"
(Hebrews 12:2 MSG).

For weeks I have been driving past a planted field trying to guess what crop would pop up from the freshly tilled ground. Soybeans were a possibility, but there were no white blooms. The stalks were too tall for squash or peas and the leaves were all wrong for peanuts. Finally, I rounded the corner one morning and came face to face with a field of giant sunflowers. The first time I had seen such a sight was in Budapest on a mission trip over a decade ago. Miles and miles of giant sunflowers on both sides of the road and their beauty was breathtaking. Now, I was again face to face with that beauty that could only come from our creative God.

While visiting Budapest, I learned that sunflowers were in the heliotrope family. This means the heads of these flowers follow the sun all throughout the day. From morning until evening, they stay focused on the sun, turning wherever it leads. I slowed the car down and soaked in the view-glowing yellow heads all watching the sun. Such an amazing display of God's handiwork.

As I drove by a few weeks later, I noticed that many of the flowers were no longer holding their heads up and following the sun. Many of the heads bent over hanging heavy with seeds. My heart filled as I acknowledged the picture before me. These flowers, who had been so focused on soaking in as much light as possible and intentionally following the sun, were now heavy with seed and they could do nothing but bow and offer their seeds to anyone who approached.

A tear snuck from the corner of my eye. Such an amazing picture of what God calls us to do as believers. We are to follow the Son and soak up His light, keep our gaze focused on Him, always turning wherever He leads. And, after we have soaked it all up, we bow and offer our filled lives to be used to nourish others.

I want to be like a sunflower. I want my life to follow Him and get so filled that I get heavy with the good stuff. The fuller I am, the more I want to bow my life and let God use me to nourish those He sends my way. Oh, how I long to be a holy heliotrope.

Prayer: Father, make me a holy heliotrope, always keeping my eyes fixed on the Son. Stir in me a desire to follow you always and teach me how to bow my life in surrender so that others may be nourished as a result of your hope inside of me.

Christy Bass Adams serves as the Outreach and Connections Coordinator at Fellowship Baptist Church in Madison, Florida. Her inspirational column, *Learning As I Go*, is featured weekly at Greene Publishing. Married, with two sons, she enjoys writing, fishing, and dirt road adventures. For more inspiration from Christy, visit christybassadams.com.

Did Mr. Rogers Say "Goodness"?

Sara C. Alsup

*"Surely **goodness** and lovingkindness will follow me all the days of my life...."*
(Psalm 23:6 NAS).

Why talk about Goodness? It spreads hope; and goodness lightens my heart. Goodness follows me all the days of my life, as sure as every morning comes. God's goodness is whispered to me in all I do. This blessing comes, not because I am good, but because He is.

Fred Rogers told the nation "to try your best to make goodness attractive."[1] He wanted his 'neighborhood' audience to realize that seeing goodness in action made a lasting influence in the hearts of 'his' children and adults. He reasoned if they saw expressions of it displayed in everyday life, they were more likely to imitate goodness in their own lives. From him, adults learned a better way to talk to children in positive ways, eliminating critical words and moderating our voice to a reasonable tone.

Mr. Rogers designed his program to teach children how to be successful by instilling in them good self-esteem, and a sense of safety and security. Goodness triumphs over evil every time. He believed children would learn that sharing felt better than bullying, that speaking kind words mattered in the heart, and that a hug gave a sense of being loved. Everyone needed these truths.

---

[1] Dr. Geffrey James, Inc.com

God's goodness guides us, protects, favors, and sustains us. Goodness is peaceful, kind, thoughtful, and it whispers loving messages into our hearts. His promises provide a firm foundation of well-being and happiness for us; they're our grace, no matter our age.

Prayer: Father, help us understand Your goodness is designed for us to embrace, enjoy, and spread to others today.

Call on Sara C. Alsup when a devotion to inspire your audience is required. She's written heartfelt devotions over ten years. When 2019 celebrated the 50th Anniversary of Mr. Rogers TV Neighborhood, she became intensely interested in his character and life and determined to write about his sayings.

MY SALT LIFE

Jackie Anders

My cat's charcoal paws climbed over my leg as I tried to read the latest message from my friend, Aria. "Hey, I want you to read something."

Aria's next words came before I responded:

> *Come with me*
> *as the water shatters your skin,*
> *your last resistance.*
> *And the harshest sky frees you.*
> *Do you hear its music?*
> *You see, no instrument shakes your soul*
> *quite like it.*
> *Quite like his voice.*

I thought, "Like whose voice?" Aria had been my friend since junior high. She never talked oddly like this, though. I typed back, "Aria, what is that about? I'm the songwriter, and I don't get it. LOL! But whose voice are you talking about? Eli's?"

No response.

I began to analyze our small exchange. Eli was Aria's last boyfriend. Maybe she was missing him. After all, Aria *had* been going through a lot because of her parents' divorce. She had become very introverted.

Tap, tap. I lifted my eyes. "Come in."

My mother stuck her head in my room. "Izzy, how was school?"

Her dark hair was pulled up into a perfect bun from her workday. Why did I resent that? Was it because she always tried to fix my hair like hers—so when we went places, we'd look like the perfect McDaniels Family?

"It was good. I'm busy, mom," I replied tersely.

"Well, good talk," she said sarcastically. "I'm making dinner. I hope you'll eat at least a little of it tonight. You need to bring up your grades. Nourishment helps."

I froze. "Mom, do you even love me? Or do you love the idea of me if I make good grades and become this perfect mini-you?"

She said nothing. She shut the door quickly.

I rolled my eyes. Aria's next message came up on the screen. "I heard it in a dream. I figured you'd like it. I know I'm not a poet. I'm not much of anything these days."

I replied, "In a dream? Tell me about it?"

A few moments passed before Aria's next and even more unusual reply came. "Sometimes I need to just get away. Disappear. Get away from this salty life. You've been a good friend."

I froze. Should I call her? I clicked Eli's message box instead. I knew he'd know what was going on.

While I waited, Kitty had jumped off my bed and bolted to the corner of my room. He stared at me before rubbing his back against my guitar. A bit of dust scattered off the strings, and I wondered about the last time I had felt the urge to play it. It had been a long time. In fact, I hadn't played since Eli moved.

Eli had been Aria's and my friend since our first year in high school. We had often gone to Galveston's public beach to swim. I remembered jumping into the warm Gulf waters with him right behind me. Aria would stay on the shore. She'd never come into the "dirty water," as she had called it.

She would stay on the sand and lay under that same multi-colored umbrella she bought when she lived at the lake up north. She always preferred freshwater to saltwater.

Thinking back, I realized that year was fun—before we gave up on the outdoors to focus on a world of "digitalized instant gratification," as my Nana called it. Those were good times. A time when I had a major crush on Eli, but Aria always had his attention instead.

Eli answered my message, "What's up?"

I replied, feeling ridiculous that I was excited to talk to him. "I'm worried about Aria. She's talking funny."

I told him what she had messaged.

"It's probably just a teen girl thing," he responded. "If you don't hear anything different tomorrow, let me know."

"Thank you, Eli."

I really needed Aria to clarify what she meant , but Eli wasn't worried. Why was I?

Eli, the boy with the perfect skin, who hid his big, blue eyes behind wire-rimmed glasses until he tossed the glasses onto the sand to swim. Why did I never get over him? He didn't like freckled-faced girls like me. He had a thing for redheads instead.

Crash! I jumped as it sounded like pots crashed on the hardwood floors of our kitchen. Mom was probably rushing through the kitchen to get dinner ready.

I looked at my computer. Nothing. Should I do school work? I started scrolling the Internet instead. I studied some images, got bored with others, and screenshot a few. Before I knew it, Mom was calling from the kitchen that dinner was ready. Where did the past hour go?

As I entered the kitchen, my mother was pouring canned sauce into a pot, and my father asked about her day.

I should have been happy. I had everything. Both parents, nice home. So why wasn't I happy? Why weren't any of my friends happy either? What is the elusive term, *happy*, anyway?

The next day, after chemistry class, I was walking through the halls when I ran into a large body. "Ms. Izzy McDaniels?"

"Yes?" I lifted my eyes to see Principal Hadley.

"Come with me," he said.

Something wasn't right. I'd never had to go to the principal's office before.

When his office door opened, I saw blue-uniformed men with badges on their shirts. My knees went weak as I collapsed into a seat. That's when I noticed my mother sitting there. Her expression was vacant. "Why is my daughter here?" Her hair pulled up perfectly, of course.

The taller cop gazed at me. "When was the last time you saw Aria Davis?"

"Why? Is something wrong?"

"There may be. And we think you know about it. Her mom found a note saying she was running away. And cameras caught images of a strange van on her road around midnight."

"And?"

"Both of you chatted online with a man named Roger Smathers. FBI data banks show he is a known child trafficker. So where is Aria?"

My mom gasped. "This is crazy. My daughter would have said something if she knew Aria was in danger."

My mother was standing up for me! I couldn't believe how good that made me feel.

"Ms. McDaniels, they both talked to him online."

I frowned. "We just chat with other teens, not a Roger."

"Let's just hope we find Aria safe. Until then, we'll be in touch," he replied.

After that bizarre meeting, my mom started monitoring my online activity. I asked, "Don't you trust me? How is this love?"

"It's tough love. The best kind," she said.

During the next few weeks, I worried about Aria, but still felt a trace of hope that Aria was okay.

Through it all, my mother and I had begun to get closer, especially the night that she handed me a letter and simply walked out of my room. I opened it and read: *You asked me if I loved you. But I didn't know what to say. I love you, Izzy, and I want you to know that He loves you more. You need Him, like I did. When I was lost, He found me as He will find you. Don't you see? I'm hard on you because if I don't do my job, how will you ever know Him? You need to know that He will always be there for you.*

Her words gave me chills. I *had* been so lost. So distracted by everything unimportant.

It was odd. My mom repeatedly capitalized the pronoun, *he*. God? I hadn't talked or heard about God since...

I rushed to my bookshelf to grab a book Nana had given me. I flipped to the first page. Sure enough, the author had capitalized *He* referring to God. Instantly, my heart told me what my mind continued to deny—I did need God. I bowed my head and prayed for both me *and* Aria.

Then came music. The melody rushed over me like a freight train. I walked to the corner of my room, picked up my guitar, and let the words come.

Won't you reveal what you've been showing?

As time eats up the pages of my story.

And every little doubt numbs my truth

and takes me farther away from You.

So when will I see past the noise?

When will I find my voice?

So that I can find You.

I hadn't written or sung in years. I laid my guitar down and smiled. I had never felt so at peace. And then to my surprise, as if in a dream, I thought I saw Aria walk through my door.

Jackie Anders is a speculative fiction author that has a Bachelor's degree in Business Management, a Master's degree in Educational Leadership from Texas A&M, and currently teaches at a public school in the Houston, Texas area. She hopes to inspire her students to use their imagination and to think 'outside the box' to uncover their creative side too. Jackie currently lives in Houston, Texas with two cats, one dog, and three kiddos!

When You Think Your Kids Aren't Listening
Michael L. Anderson

"I remember the first time I saw tears in my Dad's eyes. It was while he was telling me a story about a time he'd taken advantage of one of his friends. Even as a child, I could feel his regret for his uncharacteristically mean behavior. From hearing his story, I knew I didn't ever want to be an exploiter. His story made me a better person and more aware of others – not just that day, but for the rest of my life. It was a story passed down ... lore, if you will, which changed me."[1]

While I presented a routine family Bible lesson in our basement on a dreary Sunday morning years ago, a memory from my past dribbled out. Perhaps bitten by a nostalgia bug, I vividly recalled a specific time from my youth when I had not been nice.

My grandfather gave me an electric train for my ninth birthday. It was a shiny Silver Bullet deluxe model from American Flyer, the best brand of the day. The train set consisted of a sleek chrome locomotive engine and two matching passenger cars. I only had enough track for one modest oval, but I was content—or so I thought.

I stored my train set under my bed. Some days, I would slide it out and set it up. For hours I lived in a pretend engineer world. Watching the train go around always reminded me of my dear "Gramps." He loved me and I loved him.

---

[1] Excerpt from Folkloristic.com, a blog site authored by Bernie Michael Anderson

My friends were less interested in electric trains. They were into little plastic army men. So, to keep up, I had some army guys, too. On indoor play days, when it was snowy and cold outside, we would spend hours setting up tiny toy soldiers in various poses on the floor. We made continuous boyish soldier sounds of machine guns and bombs bursting during our imaginary war games.

During our school's Christmas break, my nearby friends were not available to play as most were out of town visiting family. I was the only kid left in the neighborhood except for Dennis Dugo. He lived across the frozen pond in a run-down house on a dead-end street.

Dennis had messy hair and wore glasses with thick "Coke bottle" lenses. His clothes looked like wrong-sized hand-me-downs. Other kids teased Dennis and, while I didn't taunt him like they did, I never stood up for him or came to his defense.

Bored without my friends, I played in the snow by myself the first day of school break. I saw Dennis in his distant backyard. I called to him and he sheepishly walked towards me. We talked a little, and then we started building a snow fort together. I asked him if he wanted to come over to my house the next day and play inside. He said he would ask his mother, but that it sounded great.

The next day we played indoors at my house. We played with my train set for awhile. Dennis remarked that he had a train set too — an American Flyer. Dennis also liked playing with my army men. He liked them so much, a devious thought crept into my mind. *Wonder if I could trade some of my army guys for some of his train set?*

I suggested to Dennis that he come over to my house again the next day and bring one of his train cars for a possible trade. I could tell he didn't like the "trade" idea, but I kept up my boyish pressure. Finally, he agreed, and the next day he brought over a boxcar that turned me green with envy. I offered him only twelve of my plastic army guys to see if he would budge. Dennis hesitated, but then told me in a quiet voice that he would make the trade ... if I would still be his friend. I agreed.

Then I encouraged him to return to his house and bring me another train car from his set and we could trade again. "That is, if you still want me to be your friend," I added.

Dennis bundled up and climbed through the deep snow across that icy frozen pond to his house. He eventually returned with another collectible train treasure. He traded again for another measly dozen of my cheap plastic army men.

I suggested to Dennis that I come over to *his* house the next day and we could make more trades. He said he would first check with his Mom because no other kids had ever been inside his house before. Keeping the pressure on, I told him I would be at his house promptly at 9:00 a.m. to trade or he could forget about me being his friend.

The next morning, with boots, coat, and gloves on, I plodded through the snow following Dennis's footprints from the days before leading to his back door. I carried a big brown paper sack filled with my remaining plastic army guys, but with enough extra room inside to carry home lots of new train cars.

I knocked on the door. Thick weather stripping seemed to hold the door together as the loose worn plastic insulation blocked any view inside the windows. Dennis pushed open the door and invited me inside.

The smells of starch filled the tiny room as I was greeted by Dennis's mom. She had stopped her ironing to welcome me. "You must be Mike. Dennis talks about you all the time."

Dennis left the room. I guessed he went to his bedroom to gather some train cars. I was alone in the dimly-lit kitchen with only his Mom ironing away. She was so pretty and had a kind voice like a princess. She wore a Christmas apron and offered me a freshly-baked cookie. With Dennis still out of the room, his mother spoke to me.

"I want to thank you, Mike, for being friends with Dennis," she said. "He likes you very much. You know, Dennis doesn't have many friends, no sisters, no brothers, or a Dad, either, so I value you as a young man who wants to be his friend for the right reasons."

She paused for a moment before continuing. "I hope that you would never be mean to him, or trick him, or take advantage of him."

An uneasy feeling came over me—one that I had never felt before. *Did she know about our lopsided trades?*

As she paused again and set her iron down, she looked over at me with a smile and gently said the words that stabbed my little heart so painfully that I can still feel it today. "You know Mike...Dennis's grandfather gave him that train set."

Oh God, what have I done? If his train meant as much to Dennis as mine did to me—because his Grandfather gave it to him—it would be priceless and not open to trade of any kind. How could I be such a louse?

About that same time, Dennis burst into the room, but with only a bag of army men. He poured them out on the floor. Without a word spoken, I poured my guys out too and we began to engage in the kindest toy war games two boys could ever have, and with minimal sound effects too.

No more talks of train trades were ever uttered. Sadly, Dennis and I never played together again after that winter day. I was too ashamed and hid my guilt inside for years.

later, I tried to locate Dennis after high school. I so wanted to apologize and ask for his forgiveness. He never returned for any class reunions. Why would he? Kids were so mean to him and so was I in my own way.

Perhaps that my grown son remembers my tears while telling this story to him when he was a boy and how he then vowed not to take advantage of people ever in his own life

... *that* can be my story of God's grace and, ultimately, a happy sort of ending.

Michael A. Anderson is a freelance contributing writer and product reviewer for various publications. His *Writing for Magazines and Going the Anthology Route* are popular workshops at writers conferences. He is an active member of Word Weavers International and is the Co-Founder of the Christian Authors Guild.

The Promise Keeper

Linda Ray Center

My cell phone woke me at four a.m. "Mom can't breathe," my sister whimpered on the phone. "An ambulance is taking her to the emergency room."

I sat up clinging to the phone, "What?"

"It's bad. You need to come home. Now."

Life is full of stressful situations. Fear and panic are subconscious reactions, feelings that arrive unbidden. Some people panic in a crisis. Others think clearly. Faith believes God is God, no matter what we are going through. Faith is not a feeling: faith is a choice.

During the seven-hour trip to the hospital, I drove high speeds, praying the whole way. *Please, Lord, remember my mom, meet her needs. Allow me one more time to tell her how much I love her.*

After I arrived at the hospital, I sprinted to the elevator and pushed the button to the intensive care unit. I found Mom lying on the bed, monitors blinking behind her, and tubes draped across her body. Our eyes locked. She nudged her oxygen mask aside. "You're here."

I dashed to her bedside and kissed her cheek. "Are you in pain?"

She shook her head.

"Can I get you anything?"

"I'm thirsty."

My brother handed me something from Mom's tray that looked like a sponge popsicle. "She can only sip on this."

I frowned.

"Doctor's orders!"

I gave my brother a weak smile and turned to Mom. She sucked on the sponge a few seconds and handed it back to me. "I'm tired. I want to sleep now."

"Okay, Mom. I'll be here when you wake up." I went to the restroom to freshen up and saw my bloodshot eyes in the mirror.

Walking back towards Mom's bed, I felt the Lord's presence. I froze and thanked Him for his grace during the drive from Florida to Georgia. The interstate and Atlanta had less traffic than usual, bringing me to Mom in time.

My sister explained the details of Mom's heart attack. She insisted I go home to rest and volunteered to spend the night in the hospital. I hugged my sister goodbye and told her I would care for Mom tomorrow.

I slumped into bed, asking God to guard Mom's heart. Through the night, I fought sleep by worrying over Mom's critical condition. Oddly, she seemed at peace. I knew her faith would play a huge part in carrying her through this difficult time. Was my faith that strong?

The story of Jesus crossing the Sea of Galilee churned in my mind. A great storm arose and waves broke over the boat while Jesus slept. The disciples were afraid, as chaos broke out, but Jesus slept peacefully. The shaken disciples woke him. "Don't you care?"

Jesus stood and said, "Peace, be still!" A great calm hovered over the waters. He turned to the disciples. "Where is your faith?"

I fell asleep asking God to increase my faith.

The next morning, I discovered Mom propped on pillows in her hospital bed. "Come in," she said. "You don't mind if I finish my breakfast?"

"Go ahead." I smiled warmly. Mom placed a bite of eggs into her mouth. "The color in your face looks much better."

"I feel better."

"How did everybody sleep last night?" I asked.

"Mom slept well. I woke up each time the nurses came in to check on her vital," my sister said.

"You can go home and grab some sleep now. I'll be here."

My sister handed Mom her milk carton. "I want to stay to hear what the doctor says."

The nurse detached a few monitors and helped Mom take three steps to a chair beside her bed. The doctor ordered a test to determine the damage to her heart. My neck muscles tightened when he explained she might need stents. *No, not stents. That meant surgery. She might not wake from the anesthesia.* I sensed a small whisper in my spirit: 'Remember the disciples despair during the storm. They never saw a storm turn so quickly into a perfect calm. Trust me. My grace is sufficient.'

After the doctor left, I asked Mom if she was scared. She patted my hand. "No, the Lord is with me. I trust the promises of peace found in His Word." I could not believe how calm she was. Mom did not like the unknown, yet she was not frightened. Anyone can trust God when everything is fine. But the test comes when we choose to trust him when we don't understand. Her trust in God was a perfect example of faith in God.

That afternoon, Mom's pastor and our family held hands to pray before the staff wheeled her from the room for the test. Afterward, I excused myself and wandered outside. On a bench, I prayed. *Forgive me for my lack of trust. My mom trusts you completely. I trust you, too, with Mom's life and in every area of my life.*

Minutes later, back in Mom's room, the phone rang. The doctor told us the test proved no permanent damage. Since her vital signs returned to normal, she would move to a private room.

After Mom woke, we gave her the latest test results. She smiled. "Nothing less than God's provision."

The next day, the doctor released Mom. While waiting for her discharge papers, she told us about the morning of her heart attack. "I felt extreme pain shoot through my chest, and breathing became difficult. I cried out, 'Help me, Jesus,' and somehow, He gave me the strength to stagger to the telephone. Jesus is a Promise Keeper. He keeps His promises even during horrendous pain. He was my present help in trouble."

I stepped out of the hospital room and turned to look at Mom. Tears threatened as I gave thanks to the Promise Keeper for His amazing grace.

Linda Ray Center is a writer and inspirational speaker. She has published *The Relationship Dance* and *Crystal Discovers The Glow*. She is also a contributing author to Abba's Answers, 2020 Florida Writers Illusion Collection, and SuperBudZ. Her work has appeared in several magazines. Linda resides in charming Chattanooga.www.lindaraycenter.com

He Didn't Push Her in the Well!

Carri Colvin

Love. What is it, and what does it mean to do it well? Long ago, in a desert land, and during the hours of the day when the heat is usually most intense, a woman made a trip to a well to draw water. Whether it was scarce and she needed to collect before the well ran dry, or she was attempting to escape the burning judgment of others for her lifestyle choices, she needed water. Was the heat sweltering? Did she attempt to hide beneath more cloth than was customary so she would not be noticed? Did sweat drip down her body and lick up the dust on her skin in muddy streaks? Was she hopeless? We don't know those details, but we do know that she met unconditional Truth in Love that day, and that Love ran much deeper than the well where they met. Soil baked hard by the intense middle-eastern sun, broken and dug deep within, certainly held life. However, this well's copious life was not within, but *at* the well. Jesus was a stranger to her; however, she was no stranger to Him. He was with her, in the flesh, having a conversation about thirst, about water. He, too, was thirsty. His physical body needed physical water. Yet, He knew a secret, and He was about to share it with her.

In my own life, I understood clearly that loving well meant that I would have to dig deep, but I couldn't fathom how painful the excavation process of my heart would be. I didn't realize that there was so much dirt in the large heart others frequently complimented. It was encouraging to hear that I was too nice, and that I saw the world through rosy colored glasses. The world was pretty in pink. I thought this made me a pretty good person. But, shallow wells make nothing more than a mud puddle.

Betrayal, especially from a loved one, can fog the rosiest of glasses. Repeated betrayal can shatter the lenses. The life-depleting efforts I put forth in discovering truth would pale in comparison to the energy I would expend trying to remain in a state of forgiveness. I began to see the world through a very different colored lens than rose. The world was now gray. I wondered if the pain would subside long enough to allow love to flow through me again, let alone love those who hurt me the most. I thought this made me a bad person. Mining for that which is pure is a painful process.

Thirsty for God's truths, I pored over the scriptures and craved being filled with a forgiveness that would pour out of me to others. I needed Him to teach me how to love. Had I ever truly loved anyone . . . *unconditionally*? I was not so certain. The dank void within my heart reeked of tremendous loss, reverberating the confessions and justifications, resounding that which was done and, at times just as painful, that which was not done. Flowing with the force of a wild river, anger, judgment, bitterness, rage, and a self-justified wrath began to fill the vacancy. However, the Word of God is not a people pleaser and will not allow us such petty pleasures. Truth dams toxic behavior and calls us back to the well, where we can trust Him to unearth all with a confidence and vision of depth, purity, and refreshment that will fill us to overflowing, a nourishment for ourselves and for others. It can be tricky for us human beings to hold the weight of Truth. It can become a burden, or that with which we burden others. It can become the club we beat others with before we toss them into the well, especially when our natural desire for vindication prevails. God's ways guide us in using truth well, and as we become more like Him the hurting become healed, and the healed learn to be healers in a hurting world. Like Jesus, we meet people at the well.

Jesus didn't push her in the well. Having four husbands, and now with a fifth man, many, especially the most "clean" would think they had just cause. Jesus saw her, understood her, spoke truth, and told her what to do. He gave her hope, and now it was her choice. Would she reject Him? Would she follow His ways? A heart baked hard by the hardships of life, broken deep-found Truth, found Life, a life that overcomes death. At the well she met the One who in the beginning split all that was in existence, water, to create the dirt she stood upon, broken through to draw a drink. The body needed what the well could provide, but only He could provide what she needed most.

Everything was water. He split the waters to create what we must split to find water. It is a curious thing to ponder that we often don't see the Water for the lakes. Do we spend more time seeking to fill the cup with which we drink to satisfy thirst for a moment, or do we bring our bodily clay vessel to Him to be filled with the Spiritual drink that washes us clean from the inside out and fuels us for eternity? It is the cloth that cleans our lenses that we may see with clarity and no hue, but a crystal clear view.

While painting makes Carri Colvin's heart beat, inspiring others to find hope in all things through picture and story makes it dance. When Carri is not writing or painting with her Maltese companion, she can be found rollerblading, paddle boarding, and biking in sunny Naples, Florida.

Elijah Heard the Whisper

Jeanie M. Connell

The story of Elijah, fearful and discouraged, wanting to end his life is found in 1 Kings 19:3-4. *Elijah was afraid and ran for his life. 4b He came to a bush, sat down under it and prayed that he might die. 'I have had enough Lord, take my life"* (NIV).

Elijah slept, and when he woke, the Lord provided food and then told Elijah, "Get up and eat."

This scene follows a courageous act to obey God and stand up to large numbers of people who did not believe in Almighty God. The location was Mount Carmel and the people wanted to follow false gods.

Elijah was accused of being a troublemaker. He felt outnumbered and alone in his belief in the Lord his God.

In 1 Kings 18:18 Elijah says, "I have not made trouble for Israel. But you and your father's family have. You have abandoned the LORD'S commands and have followed the Baals. Now summon the people from all over Israel to meet me on Mount Carmel. And bring the four hundred and fifty prophets of Baal and the four hundred prophets of Asherah, who eat at Jezebel's table." Jealous Jezebel was married to Ahab. She hated Elijah for his heroic acts and threatened to kill him.

Elijah heard the Lord speak to him several times, instructing him to eat, drink and be strengthened for his journey. Then the Lord spoke again after Elijah had spent the night in a cave saying, "What are you doing here Elijah?"

Have you ever heard the Lord ask you that question?

Elijah's response is priceless! He explains to God that he is a *good guy*. "I have been very zealous for the Lord God Almighty. The Israelites have rejected Your covenant . . . I am the only one left and now they are trying to kill me too" (1 Kings 19:10).

Have you ever tried to explain to God the reasons behind your actions? As my daughter would say, "How did that work out for you?"

This is God's response to Elijah in verse 11, "Go out and stand on the mountain, for the Lord is about to pass by."

I love it when God gives me a specific instruction. I want to find out what happens next. I think Elijah did too. He obeyed God.

God can be so dramatic. *A great and powerful wind tore the mountains apart and shattered the rocks before the Lord, but the Lord was not in the wind.*

How strange, I would've expected to hear God in that powerful wind.

Next, *there was an earthquake, but the Lord was not in the earthquake*. Elijah seems to be looking for God, expecting to find Him, without results.

After the earthquake came a fire, but the Lord was not in the fire.

During times of powerful winds, like Hurricane Michael in our local Florida beach town, many cried out to God for deliverance. During times of earthquakes in California, my sister looks for the Lord, not to mention the dramatic forest fires that leave people homeless.

In my married life we have been uprooted and moved to a new state twelve times. There is a shaking and quaking of sorts. My foundation feels uncertain. I look toward the Lord to know how to proceed and to be assured of His presence.

*And after the fire came a **gentle whisper**.* Elijah must have been listening closely to hear a gentle whisper. Immediately after hearing it, he sprang into action. He pulled his coat up over his face and stood at the mouth of the cave.

After this dramatic scene, after the waiting and watching and listening, God said, *"What are you doing here Elijah?"*

Has God ever asked you that question?

Please allow me to paraphrase the remainder of Chapter 19. Elijah reminds God of how zealous he has been for the Lord God Almighty. He feels certain that he is the only loyal servant left and now he's in danger of death.

God's response to Elijah is to send him back the exact way he came. He gives him careful instruction to enlist help through anointing specific men with specific duties. God corrects Elijah's account that he alone is faithful. *"I reserve seven thousand in Israel – all whose knees have not bowed down to Baal."*

Elijah obeys God's instructions. I suspect God knew that he would. I hope that God expects my obedience when He speaks to me.

I hope I can be counted on to listen for God's *whisper* and trust His voice. His whispers are all about grace. Always about grace. The grace I don't deserve.

We will never outgrow our need for His whispers of grace.

Jeanie M. Connell is a singer/songwriter, and psalmist who compiled her poems from personal journals in 2008. Her third CD, *I Call His Name*, of original songs was produced in 2009. Jeanie, a member of Word Weavers, just completed her memoir, *Promise You Won't Remember*. She and her husband Michael reside in Franklin, Tennessee.

Grace

Carolyn J. Fisher

Like Joseph's coat of many colors, grace also comes in many colors. Grace can be the blessing we ask before meals. It can be poise and style when we see a stylish lady walk across the room. It can be a blessing, or even forgiveness. For me, it was both a blessing and forgiveness. This was something I had to learn the hard way.

My husband died on February twelfth, two days before Valentine's Day. Because I had been a secretary in my church for ten years, members there knew me well. Yet, it had slipped by the receptionist that my husband had died. The day after his death, she called me to ask why I hadn't signed us up for the Valentine Social that Friday night. Of course, it stung. I believe she felt worse when I told her he had gone to heaven the day before. I felt bad because she felt so bad and was embarrassed. Obviously, I did not attend.

The following year, I did sign up. The fellowship would be good for me, and I always enjoyed the entertainment and being with friends. With my ticket purchased and something new to wear, I drove to our Church Fellowship Hall, planning to have a nice time. My whole life I have been early, and this evening was no different.

Standing outside waiting for the doors to open, a friend, who we had played games with sometimes, walked over and asked, "Why don't you sit at our table. I was helping decorate and I reserved it already? It's the first table on the right." I responded quickly, as I was very grateful to have someone to sit with. "Thank you for asking, and I will come over when they open the doors." She then went off to talk with someone else.

When the doors opened, I immediately went over to the table where the chairs were turned up to save places. As I reached for a chair, my "friend" came quickly to my side and said, "I am so sorry, *I forgot* we had it reserved for *couples*." I looked at her and said, "No problem at all, there are plenty of empty chairs and I am sure there will be someone to sit with." I turned and walked away with tears beginning to roll down my cheeks when another couple I knew saw me. They called out for me to come over and sit with them. After explaining my tears, they dried up quickly. It wasn't long before our table filled up and we had fun, nice evening, even though I was the only single person at the table.

This experience was part of learning to be a widow, and there were many lessons. I wish I could say I got over that one quickly, but I didn't. I carried it with me for almost a year. It was difficult talking with the lady who had hurt me, she probably didn't even realize she had. They never asked me to play games again. Now, I was no longer a *couple*, or a *pair*. I was a widow, and folks unfortunately don't know how to treat us. I felt like I had a scarlet letter on my back. The word WIDOW always makes me think of a black widow spider. Something ugly that stands out.

I was guilty of letting that hurt stay with me far too long. After praying about what I would say and how to say it, I finally decided to go to this lady and nicely tell her how she had made me feel when telling me I couldn't sit with them because I didn't have a mate. Widows have tender hearts and yes, I had been hurt, but I wanted her to know I forgave her, but most of all I wanted her to learn to tread lightly with widows. Someday, she might be one. It took a burden off me and I pray I was gracious in talking with her. She seemed to receive it well. We greet each other on Sundays with a hug and things are fine now.

Going to several Grief Share meetings, I decided they weren't for me. It must have been the ones I attended because I heard wonderful things about the organization. Now, six years later, and having been through the program three times, I can honestly say it is a wonderful organization. Apparently, I wasn't ready at the time, but now I know what a blessing it is.

But how I got there was a little unusual.

After leaving two meetings, I called my church and asked for the names of the last five women to become widows. I planned a brunch out on my deck on a Saturday morning, and asked each of them to bring a funny story about their husbands. Then I ordered a small book on widowhood to give them as a small gift when they arrived. We had a delightful time laughing, and yes, there were a few tears, but that is normal and expected. We met for almost a year. During that time, I met another friend who had some counseling experience. Our little group was growing. My friend and I decided to go to our Pastor and ask permission to meet at the church and open it up for anyone who needed to come. He was all for it. The material was ordered, they gave us a room and a time to meet. We had a few come and a few go, but all in all it was very successful.

There are ten of us who have bonded and have remained close friends. We feel that now we are on the other side—that it was the gift of grace we received from God which enabled us to get through it with Him by our sides.

We do a lot of social things together and thoroughly enjoy each other. The biggest thing we have learned is in II Corinthians 12:9 (NIV), *"My grace is sufficient for you, for my power is made perfect in weakness."* He has proved it over and over.

Carolyn J. Fisher lives in Independent living and enjoys many activities such as writing, painting, traveling, and church ministries. She is a member of Word Weavers and has written *"When You Can't, God Can"*, personal memoir; *"The Tea Set"*, Christian romance; poems for Maturity Magazine; and a short story for *"Blessings in Disguise."*

Call Answered

debi

I found myself in deep depression again. I knew my Lord thought me precious and wouldn't let anything happen to me that I couldn't handle. Yet, I felt helpless as I was hopelessly behind on bills. Circumstances after happenstances coupled with unforeseen hurdles left me breathless. I was no longer facing challenges. I was hiding under the covers.

I felt the need to pray but all I could muster was, "Lord?"

He whispered. I wrote His words immediately.

"I'm right here."

"I'm closer than you can imagine."

"I wish you knew how much I love you."

"I will never leave you."

My friend, let His words of grace heal your hurts, even the ones you pretend not to have.

After letting these words heal my innermost being, I began to form the courage to write my autobiography as a testimony for other survivors of emotional trauma, especially the life-altering kind. Today, I live with joy and anticipation of each new day. My goal is to lift sullen heads to praise.

The Ellen Gift

Carol Moesta Hamilton

Julius Rosenwald and Dale Carnegie said, "If you have a lemon, make lemonade." I say, "If God gives you a peach, enjoy it."

I asked God for a writing buddy—someone to share critiques, attend writers' group and conferences with me. God gave me above and beyond what I even knew to request.

At a Writing Success conference, I was invited to join a writers' group called Word Weavers (years before Word Weavers International arose). One of the members, Ellen List, learned I would be participating in St. David's Christian Writers' Conference. Should we room together? Of course! And we were off...

Ellen and I got to know each other better at that conference. Ellen writes with vivid detail, which brings her words to life. I enjoy reading what she creates. We work well together, and laugh often. From there our deep friendship blossomed. We've traveled to writers' conferences from Sandy Cove on the Chesapeake Bay on the East Coast to Mount Hermon near San Jose on the West Coast. Ellen is a diligent critique partner and a hearty encourager. We share rooms, travel expenses, Bible reading, prayers, and typically split a Reuben sandwich and a piece of pie.

By the time Ellen and I became friends, our eldest daughter, Lonnie, had married and moved to a Marine Corps base with her husband. Lonnie didn't believe Ellen really existed. She called Ellen my "imaginary friend" and said, "No one could love you so unconditionally, Mom."

One year, the day Ellen and I traveled home from the Mt. Hermon conference, we celebrated Lonnie's birthday by calling her. After Ellen talked to Lonnie and wished her a happy birthday I took the phone to finish our conversation. Lonnie laughed and still acted like she didn't believe me. "Nice job finding a maid to pretend to be Ellen, Mom."

Ellen loved the ruse and joking. When she and Lonnie finally met, Ellen insisted Lonnie touch her arm to feel that she is real.

Our lives continued to intertwine. Our husbands are medical professionals. Ellen and I work for their practices as bookkeeper wives. It's wonderful to have someone who understands and commiserates when the numbers don't add correctly.

Ellen's son and our son-in-law both serve in the United States military as pilots. We've prayed them through multiple trips and deployments. We became grandmothers within months of each other—mine born in Japan, and her triplets in Oklahoma. Our prayers for each other and our families increased.

As our families grew we started camping together. Our husbands have similar interests and get along well. Our kids like to be together as do our grandchildren. We and our growing families vacation together at least once a year.

Ellen's many roles in life make her interesting. She's full of surprises. On Mondays she is a hairdresser. She's also been known to create a new sculpted "do" on fellow campers. In the summer and fall she's a junior-high and varsity cross-country coach. In her past life she owned a Harley motorcycle shop. She and her husband enjoy rides on motorcycles, Jeeps, boats, and campers. She's a liturgical dancer, bell choir ringer, and joyful singer.

All I asked for was a friend to be a writing partner. God knew I would be blessed by more. I didn't do anything to deserve Ellen's friendship, or God's favor. John 1:16 says, "For from his fullness we have all received, grace upon grace." Through His grace He gave me a trustworthy friend who prays for my family and me. A friend who has cried with me and more often belly laughed. She has encouraged me in my writing and speaking career, and to live life well.

I thank God for giving me a peach of a friend and I enjoy her!

Ponder:

Do you have a desire for a special friendship or a goal you would like to achieve? Ask God if this would be good and beneficial. If so, ask Him to fulfill your wish. "Every good gift and every perfect gift is from above, coming down from the Father of lights, with whom there is no variation or shadow due to change, (James1:17)."

Remember, God delights in His children. Zephaniah 3:17 says, "The LORD your God is in your midst, a mighty one who will save; he will rejoice over you with gladness; he will quiet you by his love; he will exult over you with loud singing." How wonderful!

Carol Moesta Hamilton presents *"The Princess and the Superhero"* for children, *"Harmonious Living"* for women, plus writing/speaking classes. She writes Christian young adult novels, picture books, and non-fiction. She and her husband, Dennis, thrive in the country and serve through Global Disaster Response. Carol also learns by teaching the teen Sunday School class at her church.

Whispers of Grace

Gifts of Grace

Martha Rogers

The brilliant rays of sunlight are like the fingers stretching out to seize the possibilities of the day. I fix my gaze on You, oh God, and seek Your direction for the moments ahead. How precious is Your steadfast, unfailing love. In the stillness of the dawn, I rest and take refuge in the shadow of Your wings. In the abundance of heavenly treasure I relish in Your extravagant mercy and grace. I drink from Your streams of pleasure, for You are the fountain of life. In Your light I see rich gifts of Your beauty and goodness. Your peace settles in my heart as I trust every detail of my life to You. Magnificent are the mountains of Your righteousness. My soul longs to break through to new horizons and climb to new heights. For with You, O God, all things are possible. As You whisper to my heart sweet notes of grace, I surrender every dream and every fiber of my being to You. For You alone are God, who is worthy of all my devotion and praise.

There is no sin so great nor heart so hard that the incomparable love of God cannot forgive and heal. His whispers of grace relentlessly pursue those who are lost in pain and despair. Have you ever felt so broken that even in the grip of His grace you cannot be put back together again? Has your world been absolutely shattered as you face a debilitating illness or a devastating loss of a loved one? When our world falls apart, we can always relinquish our brokenness to the Healer of all hearts. He is the One who longs to carry our burden and restore our soul. This Jesus, the glorious Savior, is the One who knows, who cares and who is concerned about each and every detail of our lives. Nothing takes Him by surprise, and nothing is hidden from Him.

I stand amazed that the God of the universe who scattered countless stars in the galaxy and numbered every grain of sand would long to have a relationship with me. Only by His grace and mercy can I be restored and forgiven and stand before Him without blemish...pure...clean...free. He blots out every transgression and remembers it no more.

Oh friend, do you hear Him calling you? He is longing to free you, restore you, and make you whole. Come as you are to the One who loves you without limits. He will fill you with joy and peace unimaginable when you surrender your heart to him. Come.

Martha Rogers is a wife and mother of two adopted girls from China. She has a degree in music education and a Certificate in Biblical Studies. From her experience with depression, she hopes her writing will inspire others to find new joy. Her other passions include singing, drawing, and painting.

Never Alone

Sarah Schwerin

My arms crossed my chest. I shifted on the counselor's couch. For twenty minutes neither of us spoke. My eyes flitted from the framed degrees to the grey and brown books lining the shelves. The muted colors did little to calm my nerves. The therapist asked me at the start of the session what we should discuss. I opened and then closed my mouth.

Four months earlier I'd considered therapy at my university's counseling center. After a month of hem-hawing, I mustered the courage to make the initial appointment. My first counselor, although a courteous woman, focused on me with an intense stare. When she spoke to me, I bolted from her office. I trudged back to my dorm, defeated.

After another month, I began fresh with a different therapist on the staff. I talked about the fear I grew up with, the fear of my father who verbally abused my mother, my siblings, and me. I longed to tell him more, but my words were stuck in the past.

I stared at his brown loafers. "I…have…nightmares."

"Would you like to tell me about them?"

I glanced at him, then quickly returned my gaze to the grey carpet. My long brown hair shielded my face. "I keep seeing my brother…touching me." I checked his facial response. To my amazement, he showed no shock or disgust, only concern.

"I had no recollection of the incidents until about six months ago." I visualized the sunny day on the porch of my dorm when my brother asked if he might speak to me privately.

He had avoided my face, his eyes fixed on his worn skater shoes. "He told me a relative had done things to him. Then my brother, Alex, asked if he had ever done anything to me."

"No." I remembered my quick, emphatic response. "I told him he hadn't done anything wrong to me, but when I returned to my dorm room, I began to doubt my answer. When I laid down to sleep, memories assailed me. He had. My brother had sexually abused me."

I didn't elaborate about the flashbacks that had shattered my life every day since. In a mandatory chapel service, an image played on the memory screen of my mind. As the service continued, I huddled in my assigned seat, unable to listen to the words of the speaker. Afterward, I imagined my brother and me walking on the sidewalk together as Alex coerced me to never tell. I imagined the students around me who were chatting amongst themselves, were talking about me. I convinced myself they could see the vivid pictures in my mind, that everyone saw my dirt.

After I told my counselor, a small weight lifted. Pain and shame, however, still swallowed me. Over those next few months, I'd distanced myself from friends and family. I stopped returning phone calls. I declined shopping trips and movie invitations. Anger consumed me. I cut my brother out of all my photos. When I was alone, I yelled into my pillow. I wrote him letters filled with curses and filth, but never sent them. Rage fueled my jogging. I imagined my feet pummeling him. Still, the memories vanquished sleep.

During later counseling sessions, teary recollections filled the room, repressed pain scarring me afresh. Yet, one memory I couldn't bear to speak aloud remained to be exposed.

"Can you picture a safe place in your mind? A place where no one can hurt you?" the counselor asked.

I visualized a green meadow with a shimmering lake in the distance. The soft grass provided a carpet. With my knees tucked under my chin, I leaned back against a sturdy oak.

"Can you visualize God next to you?"

I hesitated. God had let the abuse happen. He didn't care about me. I didn't want him in my life.

He repeated his question. "Can you visualize God next to you?"

Reluctantly, I did.

"Can you journey to the memory?"

Mentally, I found myself alone with my brother. Chipped paint marred his door. The light brown carpet extended to every wall. Unable to stop the action, I watched the past unfold again.

Then he asked the hardest question. "Where is God?"

I looked at my brother's bed, my brother, me, powerless and small. As the act of abuse unfolded, I didn't see God. I assumed he was in heaven laughing at me.

"Where is God?"

Tears streamed down my face. "I don't see him."

"Look again."

I observed the child I had been, the girl hurt by the brother she idolized. I asked myself where God was.

Then, I saw him.

"What is he doing?"

God was beside me, holding my small hand, weeping.

"God never left me." In that moment the peace that had always eluded me, settled over me. God had been there all along. His grace had whispered to me: you are never alone.

---

*Some names and identifying details have been changed to protect the privacy of individuals.

Sarah Schwerin, a graduate of Asbury University and blogger, and has been published in Macaroni Kid and Shine Homeschool Co-Op Newsletters. She homeschools her two teenage sons and enjoys spending time with her husband of 19 years. She resides in Sorrento, Florida.

A Soft Landing

Susan P. Sloan

Football players would never step onto the playing field without a proper "suiting up" in the locker room. The padding beneath their jerseys serves to protect their bodies from the impact of hitting other players and, in many cases, the unforgiving ground. Pads don't keep the collision from happening, but they do make the landing easier.

In a similar fashion, God provides us with a spiritual padding to cushion a blow coming our way. It's happened to me twice, both times having to do with sudden unemployment. Anyone who's faced a similar circumstance knows how distressing it can be to lose your means of financial support.

The first time occurred when I was a college senior. My class schedule claimed so much of my time, and therefore my work hours dwindled dramatically. Although my boss struggled with making the decision, he couldn't justify keeping me when he had other prospects for my position.

The very morning that I learned about my dismissal, I received my "padding" in the form of a sermon in chapel service. The college chaplain expounded on his theme: God sometimes puts us in positions where we *must* trust Him. Even as my boss explained his regret at letting me go, I felt the Holy Spirit bearing me up, whispering comfort. "It will be all right, child. I've got this."

A few months later, I found another job, one that led me to meet the young man I would marry. There was purpose in the loss.

Sixteen years later, I faced a similar situation. After a dozen years at another company, the management decided to eliminate my entire department. This time my cushion was a song my brother and sister-in-law had sung in church the previous Sunday. The words of the song advised the congregation about facing adversity: "When you don't understand, when you can't see His plan, when you can't trace His hand, trust His heart."

Those words, coupled with my previous experience, carried me through the following months of fruitless job searches. Finally, I found the exact position designated for me. In the twenty years I worked there, I made lasting friendships and could at last utilize the degree I'd earned earlier. There was purpose in that loss as well because my new job helped me hone my writing and editing skills.

The greatest lesson from these two experiences is the truth I carry with me: God knows where I am; He goes before me, and He will provide any padding needed to secure a softer landing in any situation.

Sometimes He speaks through a song or a sermon. He may use a friend's counsel, or a written word crafted long before we need it. We need only listen for those whispers of grace and provision.

Previously a technical writer, Susan Sloan now combines her love of history and language by writing historical Christian fiction. She has authored several human-interest articles in local newspapers and denomination-specific publications. Susan and her husband live in Georgia where she is active in Toastmasters and Word Weavers.

Just Joy

Irene Wintermyer

"...for the joy of the Lord is your strength,"
(Nehemiah 8:1 NKJV).

When I trusted Jesus as my Lord and Savior, an amazing metamorphosis took place. The words *I believe* miraculously transformed my anxiety and hopelessness into supernatural joy, unlike anything I experienced before. Jesus knew exactly what I needed at the moment of my salvation, intoxicating every cell like a drug, eliminating any doubt of who provided the euphoric infusion.

Although I love Jesus with all my heart, I wondered why I don't always feel joyful as I did those thirty plus years ago. This curiosity prompted me to search for clarity when I stumbled across this verse, *"...looking unto Jesus, the author and finisher of our faith, who for the joy that was set before Him endured the cross, despising the shame, and has sat down at the right hand of the throne of God,"* (Hebrews 12:2 NKJV).

I mulled over this passage for a long time before appreciating its meaning. The joy set before Jesus as he hung on the cross had nothing to do with His circumstances, but everything to do with you and me. He knew His death would bring forth life, giving mankind an opportunity for redemption so we might live with Him for eternity. Jesus' love for us gave Him the strength to endure the unfathomable torture.

During my first overseas mission trip to Africa in 2004, our medical team ministered to many adults and children who lived in the bush. The drive to and from those locations were long and tortuous, dodging ditches and bouncing on miles of uneven dirt roads. On our last day, we had eight hundred people waiting in line to be seen. Some had traveled for days to reach us before we left for America. With only three of us providing care, the physical and emotional turmoil made me want to run and never look back. In fact, I swore I would never return.

Ten years later, a doctor friend at work asked me to go with his church to Africa for medical missions. Immediately, my mind recalled memories from the first trip and screamed NO, while my heart jumped with excitement and joy. He asked me to commit the matter to prayer. I'm ashamed to say that before praying, I reminded myself how much I hated Africa and never wanted to go back. To my dismay, joy leapt within me each time. In all transparency, I only agreed to pray for two weeks because I waited for God to say don't go—but no such luck.

There was no mistaking the joy of the Lord in this circumstance. Jesus led me down a path I didn't want to travel. Without His intervention I would have made the wrong decision, one based on an unpleasant experience instead of a focus on eternity. Needless to say, I was blessed by the trip and have returned to Africa twice since then. Despite my initial reluctance, I followed God's will and not my own. Through obedience and seeking His desire, the Lord's joy strengthened each step I took.

"His lord said to him, 'Well done, good and faithful servant; you were faithful over a few things, I will make you ruler over many things. Enter into the joy of your lord," (Matthew 25:21 NKJV).

I realized that joy is not an emotional response like happiness. It's more like a spiritual engine, powered by love and obedience, shifting me from neutral to drive. Not everyone is destined to travel overseas to a third world country, but maybe you are called to share the love of Jesus with a neighbor, a co-worker, or a family member. Whatever destiny awaits, let God's joy give you the fuel to move forward.

Irene Wintermyer began writing fiction in January 2019. After obtaining a degree in Theology, she felt lead to write devotionals, which are posted on thefaithfulpen.com. Her diverse background in medicine and business leadership has given her a foundation of experience to broach many matters of life.

Living Parables of Central Florida, Inc., of which EABooks Publishing is a division, supports Christian charities providing for the needs of their communities and are encouraged to join hands and hearts with like-minded charities to better meet unmet needs in their communities. Annually the Board of Directors chooses the recipients of seed money to facilitate the beginning stages of these charitable activities.

Mission Statement

To empower start up, nonprofit organizations financially, spiritually, and with sound business knowledge to participate successfully as a responsible 501(c)3 organization that contributes to the Kingdom work of God.

GPS Grant Program

GPS–Godly Positioning System—helps charities and non-profits position themselves, through our business coaching and the supply of grant funding, so they can succeed long-term in fulfilling their callings to minister to the unmet needs in their communities.

www.ingramcontent.com/pod-product-compliance
Lightning Source LLC
Chambersburg PA
CBHW071758040426
42446CB00012B/2615